My Life in My Pocket
for Preschoolers
(and those who love them)

K.L. Lewis

Illustrated by Paige Burleigh

Waterfront Press

Scan with any
smart phone
to learn more

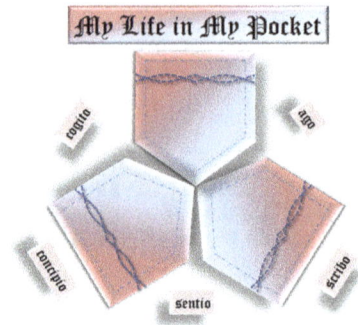

My Life in My Pocket

Published by Waterfront Publications
ISBN: 978-1-937504-31-1
WPP138P

Manufactured in the United States of America, Great Britain, or elsewhere,
when purchased outside of North or South America

Book cover designed by Paige Burleigh
Logo designed by Bertram A. Lewis, Jr., MD, PhD, MBA, FACS

Produced and distributed for
Waterfront Press by
Worthy Shorts Publisher Services BackOffice
A CustomWorthy edition

For further information contact
info@worthyshorts.com

This book is dedicated to
the parents and teachers of preschoolers—
You hold in your hugs, our future.

This is a reference book
for helping small children
to view the world as a
place of endless opportunity.

The alphabet makes all of the words that create my life.

Aa	Bb	Cc	Dd	Ee	Ff	Gg
Hh	Ii	Jj	Kk	Ll	Mm	Nn
Oo	Pp	Qq	Rr	Ss	Tt	Uu
	Vv	Ww	Xx	Yy	Zz	

Thinking creates my life!

It is never too early to begin thinking about your child's future. From the time your child is conceived, you should begin thinking about how this new generation will improve. Children should further your family in education, service, planet care, and giving. Each generation should set out to make improvements in themselves and the world at large. The expectation of success and growth for your child must be as much embedded in your thinking as is health and safety. Begin thinking of ways to develop your child's confidence, self-esteem, awareness of surroundings, awareness of behavior, and their awareness of *their* thinking. This will help your child to see the world as a place of wonder and endless opportunity.

How to Use This Book

As you read this book, let your child think about the answers to the questions. If he or she is unable to think of an answer, tell your child to "sleep on it"—or to think about it—until they come up with an answer—any answer. This will encourage the practice of problem-solving through thinking, thus helping your child to exercise their decision-making ability. If your child does not have an answer to the question just now, save the question for another time. Don't try to define every word listed under each letter unless your child asks for its meaning. These words are an introduction to the many more words they will learn as they grow older.

The questions are asked in a way to get the child to turn inwardly and think. Some questions are formed using the word "my" instead of the word "your." For example, instead of their reading or hearing you state the question, "What is your favorite color?" the question states "What is my favorite color?" This internalizes the thought response.

Read the question aloud and then you go ahead and answer the question first; after that, have your child provide his or her answer. This will cause the question to be framed in the form of self-talk. Have your child include drawings as part of their answer or have them write words that describe what they are thinking and, perhaps, what goals they are trying to achieve.

If your child needs help to write, hold your hand over the hand that holds the pencil and help them to write or draw their answer. Don't worry about the content of what your child may say or draw, simply let your creative child show his or her creativity through thinking.

Read each day and your child's ability to think will grow just as their bodies have grown. Be sure to tell your child about the things *you* enjoyed as a child. Introduce some of your *own* words for discussion. This is great practice for exchanging ideas with your child to help to build ongoing conversations between you and your children as they grow on to the less communicative teenage years.

At the bottom of each page are suggestions to you, the parent, to help you to promote within them the process of thinking as a method to resolve questions. The first word in each group is meant to create an overall positive outlook as it relates to thinking.

Note that the pocket person shown on each page does not necessarily describe the main word discussed on that page. It shows another concept that begins with the letter on that page and provides another opportunity for discussion and exploration with your child.

Enjoy this time with your child—enjoy *and facilitate* their thinking because thinking precedes action; if their thoughts are good, their behavior will be good!

Go to www.MyLifeInMyPocket.com with your child for additional play and learning. Click on "Book Series" and then "Preschoolers."

Achievement, action, athletic, America, able **A a**

Aa is for achievement.

I can do many things.

What can I do today?

What can I do tomorrow?

What can I do this week?

A—My name is Anna.
I come from Afghanistan and
I sell apples.

Parent Suggestion: Ask your child what they did today. What did they do that was successful? What do they want to do this week? At this age children have many goals: they want to memorize the alphabet, write their name, dress themselves, learn their parent's cellphone number and address—and lots of other important things!

B b

Beautiful, bright, bold, big

Bb is for beautiful.

I am *beautiful*.

What is *beautiful* about me today?

B—My name is Bethany.
I come from Baltimore, and
I love beautiful butterflies.

Parent Suggestion: Ask your child what they think is beautiful in general. What makes something beautiful? Then ask them what they think is beautiful about themselves; what about other people they know? What makes them beautiful? Discuss the importance of seeing beauty in everything around them; big things *and* little things.

Caring, contact, confidence, capable

C c

Cc is for caring.

I *care* about the world.

What in my world do I *care* about today?

C—My name is Carl.
I come from California and
I care about carbon-free
electric cars.

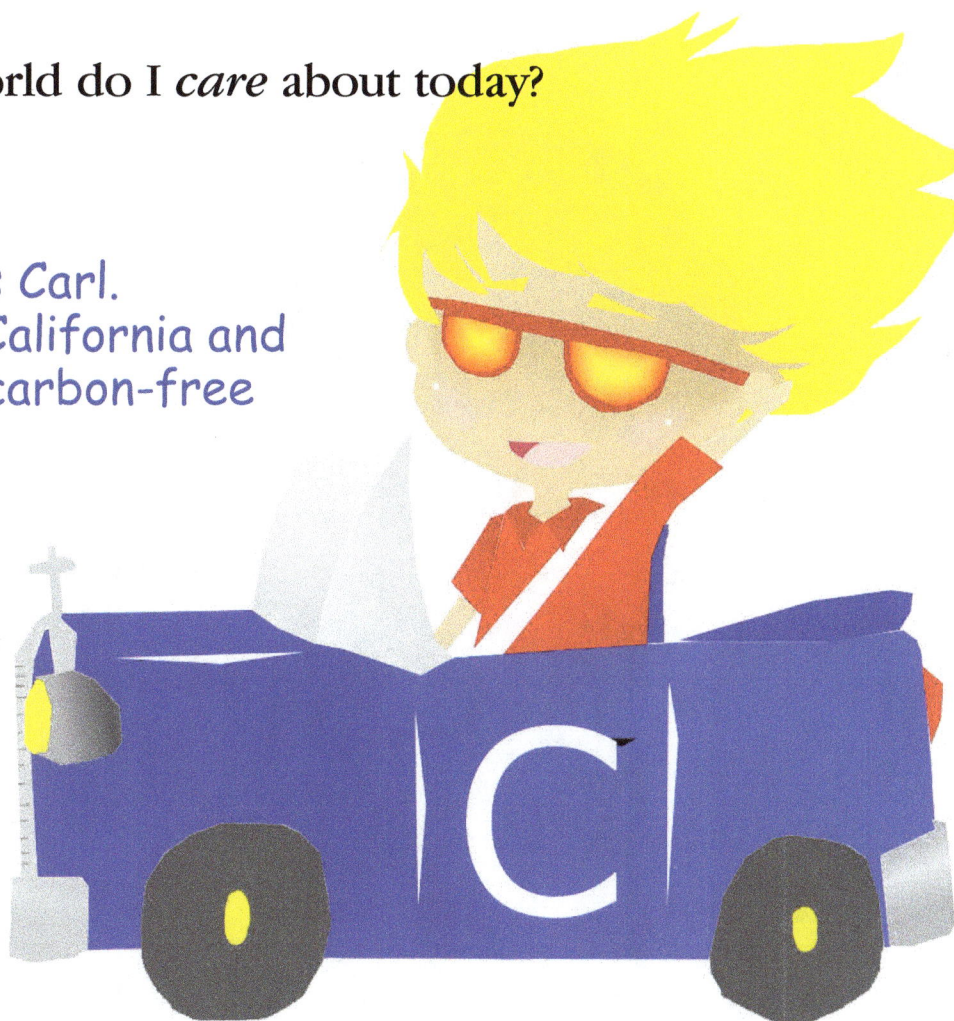

Parent Suggestion: Talk about recycling, trees, animals, and the many varieties of people in the world. Tell them what you, as both a parent and an adult, care about in the world. Introduce "caring concepts" that lead to growth and understanding.

D d

Dd is for daydream.

I *daydream* about my future.

What *daydreams* did I have today?

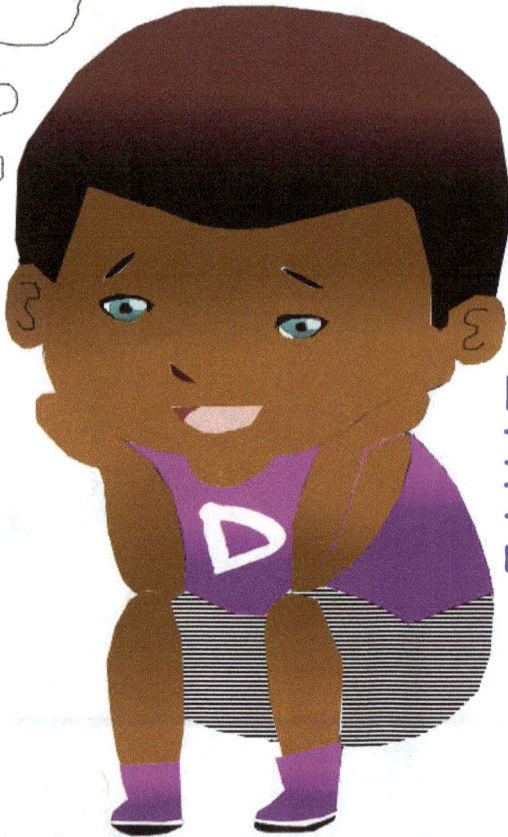

D—My name is David.
I come from Darfur and
I daydream of Daddy driving
me to get donuts.

Parent Suggestion: Ask your child about their future; what they want to have, do, and be when they grow up. Allow your child to think freely and widely. Don't judge what they say. Respond encouragingly to any answer. A small child might say that he or she wants to be, say, "cotton candy." That's more than okay because they will be loved by many!

Earth, energy, easy, effort   **E e**

Ee is for Earth.

I live on the planet *Earth*.

The *Earth* is round.

What do I love about the planet *Earth* today?

How will I care for the *Earth* now
and when I grow up.

E—My name is Earth. It's easy
for me to revolve around the sun
because something called gravity
helps me to do that and solar
energy keeps me warm.

Parent Suggestion: Ask your children what they love about being
outside – the grass, the weather, smells, other people. Tell them *your*
favorite things about Earth.

F f

Favorite, fantastic, fruit, fun

Ff is for favorite.

I have many *favorite* things.

What are my *favorite* things today?

F—My name is Frank.
I come from Fairfax and
my favorite fruit is feijoa.

Parent Suggestion: Ask your child to tell you about their favorite things and why they like them. Ask about their favorite toy, food, color, friend, TV show, etc. Try to get them to explain why these things are preferred over others. Over time you will get to know your child very well.

Games, good, great, gentle **G g**

Gg is for games.

I love to play *games*.

What are my favorite *games* today?

G—My name is Gladstone.
I come from Greenland and
I gather great books.

Parent Suggestion: Talk about a particular game you created that you play with your children. If you don't have a game of your own, work with your child to create one. Our game was "Tickle Ball." We would pretend to make an invisible ball that was filled with tickles and throw it at each other. Some tickle balls were large but even the tiny ones were very effective. Our children would laugh endlessly.

H h

Happy, helpful, heaven, horse

Hh is for happy.

I am *happy*.

I have a *happy* family.

What makes me *happy* today?

H—My name is Holly.
I come from Holland and
I am happy when I ride horses.

Parent Suggestion: Tell your child what makes you happy; things like watching them while, without being asked, they put their dinner plate in the sink, being kind to a friend, or taking care of their pets. Promote kindness and independence!

Intelligent, incentive, ice cream, independence **I i**

Ii is for intelligent.

I am intelligent.

I am intelligent because I can think good thoughts.

What did I think about today?

I—My name is Isabel.
I come from Israel and
I have many incentives to be
independent.

Parent Suggestion: Speak in broad terms and be creative when discussing what your child learned today. They learn from everything and from every experience. Tell your child what *you* learned today. For example, "Today I learned that not every star is a sun." (Be ready to explain why that is true.) Having them discover that even you don't know *everything* reinforces the fact that learning is a life-long process.

J j

Joyful, jump, jam, justice

Jj is for Joyful.

Joy is a good feeling.

What made me feel *joyful* today?

J—My name is Jamie.
I come from Jakarta and
I jump with joy when
I jam with my band.

Parent Suggestion: Help your children to think about those times when they feel joy. For example, there are those times when you see joy on their faces as they run in the park, hear happy music, or when grandma, a friend, or a favorite relative stops by.

Kind, kindness, kitty, kite

K k

Kk is for kind.

I am kind.

My friends are kind.

What did I do to show kindness today?

What can I do tomorrow to show kindness?

K—My name is Kat.
I come from Kenya and
I am kind to my kitty.

Parent Suggestion: Talk about the many ways one can show kindness: for example, helping a younger sibling; comforting a child on the playground who is hurt; apologizing for an accident or mistake; or treating animals with kindness.

L l

Ll is for laugh.

I love to *laugh*.

What did I *laugh* about today?

L—My name is Lydia.
I come from Lithuania and
I love to laugh out loud.

Parent Suggestion: Think of something humorous that happened today. Talk about what makes those things funny. Talk about the differences between funny and sad.

M   m

Mm is for Mommy.

I love *Mommy.*

Mommy is kind.

What did I show to *Mommy* today?

M—My name is Marvin.
I come from Monaco and
I love to look at the moon.

Parent Suggestion: Talk about the wonderful ways he or she helped you today. Say how grateful you are for their help. Tell them how you used to help *your* Mom and how you continue, even still, to be of help to your mother. Discuss how mosquitos are annoying and how they relate to annoying things in life, like heavy traffic. Be sure to highlight the importance of staying focused on the positive and that negative things eventually dissipate just as the itching from a mosquito bite dissipates.

N n

Noise, never, night, neat, need

Nn is for noise.

I made lots of noise *today.*

What noise did I make *today?*

N—My name is Nathan.
I come from Nepal and
I like nighttime in
New York because it
is always noisy.

Parent Suggestion: Talk about different sounds. Include silence as a sound and the sound of their inner voices. Intuition is a kind of "sound." Give them examples of intuition—like how you knew whether they would be a boy or a girl even before they were born.

Opportunity, open, outside, old   **O o**

Oo is for opportunity.

Opportunity is a part of my life.

I create *opportunity* with my good thoughts.

I can be anything when I grow up.

What do I want to be when I grow up?

O—My name is Otto.
I come from Ottawa and
I offer opportunity
to others.

Community Service

Free Books

FREE Free clothing

Free Supplies

Freeclothing from my life in my pocket

All free

Free clothing

free supplies

FREE

free things

free

Parent Suggestion: Tell them that they can have, do, or be *anything* they want to be. Even if you don't believe this yourself, tell them anyway. Telling *them* will help *you* to believe! Also, the word "old" can lead to a discussion about death.

P p

People, property, purpose, performance

Pp is for people.

I see lots of *people* each day.

Who did I see today?

Who would I like to see?

P—My name is Paige.
I come from Patagonia and
I practice painting pictures.

Parent Suggestion: If you did not go out today ask them about characters or people they may have seen in books or on TV. Prompt them to think about the character of the people they've met and the people they see in the media. Ask them to tell you what they think about the character of the people they see.

Quiet, quality, quake, quit

Qq is for quiet.

I need *quiet* time every day so I can think.

I think good thoughts when I am *quiet*.

What good thoughts did I have today?

What good thoughts will I have tomorrow?

Q—My name is Quincy.
I come from Qatar and
I spend quality time with my guitar.

Parent Suggestion: Talk about the importance of thinking good thoughts and feeling good. Good thoughts and good feelings are the fuel for success.

R r

Read, remember, rich, running

Rr is for reading.

I love to *read*.

What is my favorite book today? Is it this book?

What kind of book would I like to *read* tomorrow?

R—My name is Remington.
I come from Russia and
I read to learn facts and
I run to relax.

Parent Suggestion: Your child may have several favorite books but ask him or her to choose among them for *today's* favorite book. Choosing a favorite book for today helps to build decision-making ability. Expand on this by drawing a character from the book or expressing a visual concept about the book if it doesn't have individual characters.

Success, school, search, star, shadow **S s**

Ss is for success.

I am *successful*.

What did I do *successfully* today?

S—My name is Shelly.
I come from Seychelles and
I search for stars in the
shadows of the sky.

Parent Suggestion: Talk about what your child accomplished today.
Maybe it was pouring their own milk or juice, or helping you to fill
the dog or cat's water bowl or using the bathroom independently.
Be sure to encourage equally, not just *good* behavior, but *successful*
behavior.

T t

Teacher, talk, team, tough

Tt is for Teacher.

Everyone is a *teacher*.

Who *taught* me today?

What did I learn from each?

T—My name is Tony.
I come from Tonga and
my teacher taught me that
tigers are tough.

Parent Suggestion: Even if your child does not yet attend school there are teachers everywhere: from neighbors to TV shows; from store owners to floor-sweepers. Discuss who taught them something today—maybe a sibling showed off how to put on and take off a seat belt or a neighbor's child was learning to ride a bike.

28

Umbilicus, universe, umbrella, upset U u

Uu is for umbilicus.

Umbilicus is another word for bellybutton.

Where is my bellybutton?

My body and my *umbilicus* belong to me.

How will I take care of my body today?

U—My name is Ursula.
I come from Ukraine and
I am beginning to understand
the universe.

Parent Suggestion: Talk about how their bellybutton was the life-line connection when they were in Mommy's tummy. Tell your child that the world and Mommy are very happy now because they are in it.

V v   Voice, victory, valedictorian, violin, veracity

Vv is for voice.

I love my *voice*.

Everyone has a *voice*.

What did I talk about today?

How will I share my *voice* tomorrow?

V—My name is Victor.
I come from Vancouver.
When I play music
my violin becomes my voice.

Parent Suggestion: Talk about indoor voices versus outdoor voices. Discuss how louder volume is acceptable while outside or should they or someone else need help. Tell them to use a very strong, very loud voice when they need help or feel threatened. Have them practice yelling "HELP!"

Work, water, wish, will **W w**

Ww is for work.

I like to work.

What work did I do today?

What work will I do tomorrow?

What work will I do when I grow up?

W—My name is William.
I come from Williamsburg and
I win when I work because
I work willingly.

Parent Suggestion: Did your child pick up their toys, or a piece of paper from the floor, or put their dinner plate in the sink, or practice saying the alphabet or counting to 100? These things are all part of the work that children should do daily. (Do not suggest that learning is *"work"* or that work is not fun.)

X x

Xx is for x-ray.

An *x-ray* is a picture of the inside of my body.

It is painless.

Did I ever get an *x-ray*?

Who do I know that may have gotten an *x-ray*?

X—My name is Xavier.
I come from Xochimilco and
I like how Superman has x-ray vision.

Parent Suggestion: Talk about x-rays and how they are painless. Children often break bones. Ask your child if they know anyone with a cast or who has had a broken bone and needed a cast. Explain how the body can mend itself.

Talk about people you know who work at a hospital or clinic or someone you know that may be an x-ray technician or radiologist. Talk about x-rays or other image-taking devices like MRI, CAT, or PET scan with your child and look up these devices on the internet. Talk about the bones in their bodies.

To help clarify the language, explain that there are not many words that begin with the letter "X". On the other hand, there are many words that begin with the sound "X," like excellent, excitement, exceed, exercise, and many more.

Yummy, yesterday, yearn, yes

Y y

Yy is for yummy.

Fruits, vegetables, and water are *yummy* for my tummy.

What is *yummy* today?

Y—My name is Yolanda.
I come from Yonkers and
I say yes to today,
I yearn for tomorrow, and
I never worry about yesterday.

Parent Suggestion: Talk about tastes that your child enjoyed today. Discuss the various foods that they had at each meal. Describe something that was yummy for *your* tummy today.

Z z

Zz is for zoo.

I like the *zoo*.

What is the name of the last *zoo* I visited?

What animals did I see at that *zoo*?

What *zoo* would I like to visit? Where is it?

Z—My name is Zelda.
I come from Zaire and
I zip through the zoo with
zeal. Zowie!

Parent Suggestion: If your child has not yet been to a zoo, talk about a zoo *you* would like to visit; like the zoo in Anchorage, or the one in St Louis where they have 18,000 animals: Google each zoo. If you're unfamiliar with computers, the librarian will help you to use the internet at your local library.

Read this book and discuss the pocket people every day and your child's imagination will grow every day.

About the Author

Kathy Lynn Lewis is a leading expert on Self-Advocacy. She has devoted the last fifteen years to helping families with children with special needs to advocate for their children. She travels around the country speaking and leading seminars that help individuals and businesses achieve success through goal-setting and outlining "what they want to have," "what they want to be," and 'what they want to do."

She is the CEO of My Life in My Pocket, Inc. a company that helps students, businesses, and individuals realize their potential by understanding what Earl Nightingale states: "We become what we THINK about"—and that the impossible takes a little longer, *but not much*. Ms. Lewis is the author of the *My Life in My Pocket* book series (www.MyLifeinMyPocket.com). She lives with her husband and two daughters in Tampa, Florida.

Scan with any Smartphone to learn more